VEGETARIAN FEAST WITH PLENTY OF OPTIONS

Vegetarian Recipes that are vibrant and tasty

Lillian D. Guy

Contents

1. Hello Casey here   1

2. Seaweed Sambal   5

3. FRIED GLASS NOODLE   7

4. FRIED GLASS NOODLE   11

5. PORTOBELLO MUSHROOM IN SALT AND CHILLI   15

6. AUTUMN STIRFRIED WITH SUMMER HEAT   17

7. WHITE BEAN IN TOMATOES SAUCE   21

8. LIGHT COCONUT MILK CURRY   25

9. LIGHT COCONUT MILK CURRY   37

10. MUSHROOM IN BARBECUE SAUCE   39

11. MY DIGESTION AID   49

12. VEGAN ZUCCHINI NOODLE TOM YAM   53

Chapter One

Hello Casey here

My childhood friends given me nickname Casey so you can call me Casey, for now I am settling in Madrid, originally I am come from Jakarta Indonesia. Food is always close to my heart, cooking is the way I expressed and something that very personal to me, so I would apologizing up in the front if there are any traditional recipe that I would adapt into my personal suiting.

While traveling, writing and photography is my other passion that I start to dig deeper, thankfully they are all related to each other. This book will covered all of them, my Travel story, my personal free style writing and some piece of food photography. Also in every recipe I would tried to delivered short story behind the recipe. So let's have fun with me.

I am not consider my self as vegetarian or even more vegan, but I love the piles of fresh vegetable, fruit and trying to be more conscious of my eating habit. I just falling in love with so many flavors I found on my so far exploration into vegetable and fruit land. Can you compare the burst of flavor of fresh and tasteful vegetable with some piece of meat? I no longer think twice on which I would rather to choose. Owh yes I love bloody steak but just have it occasionally, up when my body really need it, I got health situation that made me have it occasionally, owh of course there are workaround in plant based meals, but my situation usually need me to have it right away. Hence I gave this book title "Flexible", you could freely change all the protein plant based from this book, into your protein of your choice.

In this book, I think mostly you would find plant based food recipe, with my twist. I love traditional recipe but I always curious and trying to twist it, *please forgive me the traditionalist, I have a huge respect toward traditional food legacy, and there is no better way to execute classics recipe by done it as classic as possible.

I think you will rarely find me writing my Indonesian delegacy which most of them usually are meaty based and complicated, as I not really drawn into complicated. BUT there a big but here, I have some mission to slowly converted the meaty based food into beautiful dishes that are vegan friendly and more healthier *finger cross I would try my best., I hope would be my next book. I love to adapt vegetarian food because they are mostly fresh, natural, healthy, and are my family preference, do you hungry yet?

So this book would be the channel of how I express my passion on cooking, travelling, writing and photography, diary to documented my experiment and creating new adventure for myself, exploring new ingredient and places that I'd discover during my journey.

So welcome to my book, I hope you loving and enjoy this book, also I hope you find this book useful, send me a message if you want to OR if you living in MADRID lets catch up sometime, I love wandering and get lost in a city. Please enjoy

BASIC INGREDIENTS

possibilities of Terasi/Balachan substitute, that is using seaweed, very interesting idea.

Chapter Two

Seaweed Sambal

Then when the curiosity was itchy enough and I tested that idea, I used small dried Wakame or dried seaweed.

The result was like exploding sea flavor in my mouth, which quite literally explodes because the sambal was fiery hot. Now this sambal is become staple in my fridge, basic seasoning for any spicy noodle and nasi goreng. To be honest the flavor is quite refreshing.

Here below is the recipe. Ingredients the water.

2 French shallot (4-5 small shallot)

1 big garlic

1 tbsp. dried wakame or dried seaweed; soaked in 50ml water, don't throw

1/2 medium size tomatoes roma (choose the very ripe one)

1 hand-full bird eye chilies (or adjusted according your preference).

1 tsp. sea-salt

1 tsp. sugar

1 tbsp. vegetable oil

How to

Blend all ingredients together (in food processor or blender), along with water that used to soak the seaweed. Blend until smooth or according your preference.

In medium heat and medium pan, put inside the sambal, cooked until all the liquid evaporates.

When all the liquid evaporates, put inside the oil, cooked until it bubbling. Then put inside sea-salt and sugar.

Stir it thoroughly, the sambal will get darker, and that is the sign it is ready and cooked.

Keep in airtight container.

The sambal can be used as condiment or base for Nasi goreng or Fried noodle or stir- fried or experiment yourself.

I used this sambal as a companion for Nasi Uduk from previous chapter

Chapter Three

FRIED GLASS NOODLE

This chapter is still continuation from previous chapter, my favourite Nasi Uduk. Even- though specifically this food is not everyone favorite in the house, but for me it is a comfort food.

Like my collection of warm blanket, which give me protection from my own meltdown, or that kind of things he-he. I tried to not put consolation on food, I could say arrogantly that I don't have tendency on certain addiction, which I hope not on any my future. I would only say food are like remedy which work for me anytime, to walk on memory lane of my child hood, to satisfied my curiosity, to cure my boredom by experimenting, and on and on.

To make some excuse of making Nasi Uduk or turmeric rice is to enjoy this fried noodle (whether it rice noodle or normal one) . The basic ingredients are similar to my fried noodle, I think I posted somewhere in my blog.

Here as follow are the recipe.

FRIED GLASS NOODLE

INGREDIENTS

150 gram rice noodle, soaked in hot water until soft and rinse it in cold water.

1 big size shallot, slice it

3 garlic cloves, slice it

1/2 celery stalk, trim and remove the hard fiber then slice it

Few spring celery leaves, slice it

1 carrot, slice it julienne

1 scallion, slice it (separate white and green part)

1 tbsp. vegan stir fried sauce

1-2 tbsp. sweet soy sauce (replace with 2 tbsp. light soy sauce and 3 tsp. brown sugar)

Sea salt and pepper HOW TO

In medium heat and medium pan, put inside shallot, garlic, celery stalk and white part of the scallion, sautéed until soften then put inside the carrot, continue stir until the carrot soften too.

After everything soften put inside the rice noodle and all the seasoning (vegan stir fried sauce, sweet soy sauce or the substitute, sea salt and pepper. Be careful of the salt amount, since the soy sauce is salty enough, better give it a taste and add gradually). Don't forget to give it a taste and adjusted accordingly.

Chapter Four

FRIED GLASS NOODLE

Lastly sprinkle with celery leaves and green part of the scallion. Stir and thoroughly one more time until everything mix perfectly, and then take out from the heat.

Ready to serve

PORTOBELLO MUSHROOM IN SALT AND

CHILLI

This chapter is all about autumn, bare with me, as autumn is in our front door, meaning mushroom are abundant too.

Mushroom are one of my favorite ingredient, my most favorite is shiitake mushroom, with Portobello in second list, both are meaty not meaning having taste like meat but it is chewy with plenty of "meat" to enjoy. Shiitake have some specific savory, umami flavor that I can not explain, if I want to boost some hidden extra flavor, I always used this mushroom as one of ingredient. As for Portobello, I love it for it juiciness and versatility, it depend on how you seasoned the mushroom, so whatever you put on this Portobello, it will carried the flavor greatly. Usually I always have shiitake in my fridge, and for the rest of mushroom, I love them in any way.

This recipe are hot-hot-hot, if you can't handle extreme hotness, please just do add some chili according your preference. This is garlicky, salty and spicy, with hint of sweetness to balance (I do add some of sugar to balance the kick from all of those spice). But really-really simple to make, and to enjoy too, he-he, only in one blink it is gone for me.

With only few ingredients you need, it is suitable for you speedy meal, eat with warm rice, slice of avocado, simple yet satisfying for you weekdays dinner. I serve this mushroom with rice and spring onion from my kitchen scrap that I grow in windowsill.

SO shall we?

PORTOBELLO MUSHROOM IN SALT AND CHILLI

SERVE 2 small portions as complimentary INGREDIENTs

300 Gram Portobello mushroom, slice it 3 garlic clove, chop it fine

4-5 red chili, seed in, slice it Generous amount of sea salt 1 tsp. sugar

Pepper to taste

1 tbsp. vegetable oil/light olive oil 1 scallion to serve

HOW TO

In hot medium size pan and medium heat, put inside the vegetable oil, garlic and chili. Sautéed until fragrance and the garlic are slightly golden.

After the spices are fragrance put inside the mushroom and seasoned with sea salt, pepper and sugar. Stir it through and don't forget to give it a taste, corrected accordingly.

Continue to stir until mushrooms are soft but not overcooked (mushy mushroom are not attractive he-he).

Take out from the heat and ready to serve.

I serve mine with warm rice; sprinkle of another dried chili and slice of scallion.

AUTUMN STIRFRIED WITH SUMMER HEAT (VEGETABLE STIR FRIED IN CHILLI AND

SWEET BASIL PASTE)

Yeayy, my season are finally coming, I am feeling like an animal that woken up when it season to live are coming, mostly I was autopilot during all summer, sluggish and unproductive creatively, It is easily crushing to live in cyber world on now days, when the society rushing you to keep going, to run in a fast pace of world that never enough. While you know your body need to break and most importantly deserve to break.

Hoaammm for whatever it is, I just woke up from my sleep, so excuse me for any weird words.

When you go to foreign grocery shop or any shop that un-usual for you, tried and take your time to see what do they have, sometime you will find something new, something that you never know or taste before, something that off your palate, something that you are going to learn to like it. Even though in case of this recipe, I do know, I love Thai food, for any kind of them (Just yesterday I know, that there such ingredient called tomatillo, which it is look like tomato but have soft cover skin).

Chapter Five

PORTOBELLO MUSHROOM IN SALT AND CHILLI

Maybe this recipe is not practical for you, because maybe you will find a difficulty to find the paste, but you can steal the idea. You can put any Thai inspired paste as an idea to replace it and play it as you please. For the rest of the recipes are only easy classic ingredients.

I have shiitake, Portobello and zucchini. You can put any vegetable you love.

I enjoy with fragrance fluffy jasmine rice and this vegetable stir-fried, also traditional Indonesian garlic chili, I feel like being transfer into rice field in afternoon warm breeze, while I sitting freezing in my sofa enjoy it. Such a beautiful paradoxical setting, isn't it?

Chapter Six

AUTUMN STIRFRIED WITH SUMMER HEAT

(VEGETABLE STIR FRIED IN CHILLI AND SWEET BASIL PASTE)

Serve 2 Portions INGREDIENTs

1 tbsp. chili and sweet basil paste

5 red bird eye chili

green chili, seed out and slice it 1 shallot, dice it

clove of garlic, crush and chop it roughly

2 spring onion, slice it (separate between white and green part, white as a sautéed, green as sprinkle lastly)

2 spring of cilantro, stalk to sautéed and chop leaves to serve. 1 small zucchini, slice it as you please

Hand-full (4-5) shiitake mushroom

Hand-full of small Portobello mushroom, slice it half 1 tbsp. vegetable oil

Sea salt and pepper to taste HOW TO

In medium size pan and medium heat, put inside the oil, shallot, garlic, bird eye chili, chili paste, white part of spring onion, cilantro stalk. Sautéed until fragrance.

When it fragrance put inside all the vegetable, sautéed for a while, season with sea salt and pepper.

Continue to stir, don't forget to give it a taste, the paste are already being seasoned so be careful on how much you put the salt. Don't cooked too long to maintain their texture.

Sprinkle with green part of spring onion and chop of cilantro leaves. Then take out from the heat.

Ready to serve, you can enjoy it as it is or with rice.

WHITE BEAN IN TOMATOES SAUCE

This dish is something simple to enjoy, quick, light and tasty.

This was like my go to lazy recipe, with some few ingredients and quick cooking. But first of all, I am so sorry for my rambling, I just back from my spring-summer, with freeze tongue because of very minimum used he-he, you know the feeling when you are not having had quality talking with anyone and suddenly you want to talk, It feel like I am vomiting alphabets, that is the best way I describe my feeling.

It was all by myself morning, sitting alone at home. It is my favorite time when I able to devour myself, tranquilly. As I grow older, I learn to be able to appreciate my alone time; to not socializing, it doesn't mean I am anti social, and I just indulge of being quiet. Ah heavenly time.

Chapter Seven

WHITE BEAN IN TOMATOES SAUCE

Back to this recipe, you can use any kind of bean, But I choose white bean because of it

neutral flavor, creamy and ready to be blend deliciously with other ingredient, so I love it for it versatility.

I used ready to cooked bean – a.k.a. bean from the jar, I am not ashamed, it is nutritious and practical, again this are lazy recipe for me he-he. But my suggestion is to rinse the bean with cold water, otherwise would be there are acid traces of flavor, unless you like it that way, so you can do anything you'd prefer.

So shall we, get up to the kitchen?

Serve 1-2 portion INGREDIENTs

250 Gram white bean (cannellini bean), rinse it with cold water

1 garlic

Pinch of oregano only to taste

100ml light tomatoes sauce (I used from the jar too, here in Spain, we have Tomatoes Fritos, which is tomatoes blend with onion, deliciously ready to used)

100ml water

1/2 tsp. sea salt

Pinch of pepper only to taste

1/2 tsp. sugar to cut the acidity of the tomatoes – optional all depend on your preference

1 tsp. olive oil HOW TO

In small skillet or pan, and medium high heat, put inside the olive oil garlic. Sautéed until the garlic fragrance and slightly golden – keep an eyes on it, it is golden not burn.

When the garlic is fragrance, put inside the tomatoes sauce and the water, wait a minute until it bubbling, then season with oregano, garlic, pepper and sugar. Stir it well through.

Lastly put inside the white bean, stir it for 3-5 minutes until it absorb the seasoning but you have to keep an eye on it.

When the sauce is coating the white bean, taking out from the heat and ready to enjoy.

I enjoy mine with slice of avocado, chili flake and slice of spring onion.

DINNER

Chapter Eight

LIGHT COCONUT MILK CURRY

There are so many curry recipes in Asia, it maybe carried the same name, but the main spices mixes are all completely different. Let alone in Asia, we in Indonesia have so many different versions.

I will mention some that I knew, Padang curry and Javanese curry (even in Java itself there are so many version differ by the spices that used, I'd dare to say every household have different recipe).

But here I made Indian version with daring used of exotic spices, but I wouldn't dare to claim it authenticity, since I used spices mix from the jar *sigh he-he.

I don't particularly like heavy spices mix, so I just put small amount of the paste just to infuse and have some hint touch of Indian food. Hence "Light" title come from, But I love the hint of this warm bowl Indian curry, not to over power freshness taste of the veggies.

My husband tried to add amount of veggies portion onto his daily intake, with that personal request, more than happy to create one for him, and him not being picky eater, I could freely create what I please he-he.

What I love about this curry is, I can add anything that accessible for me, any seasonal local

ingredient that usually fresh and cheap. Which in this recipe consists of paprika, easy courgette and mushroom. You could create easy one for you.

Here you go

LIGHT COCONUT MILK CURRY

INGREDIENTs

1 medium courgette, half, and slice it according your preference

1 king oyster mushroom, slice (this one is what I got, you can freely used other mushroom)

1/2 paprika, square, or slice according your preference

1 shallot, slice it

Thumb size ginger, crush it

1 tsp. full of mild Indian curry paste

Few spring coriander leave to serve (don't throw the stalk, to put it inside the curry)

Sea salt, sugar and pepper

500 ml light coconut milk

700 ml water

1 tbsp. vegetable oil HOW TO

In medium size pot and medium heat, put inside the vegetable oil, curry paste, shallot and ginger, sautéed until the shallot soft and the curry paste come together with other ingredient.

After the basic ingredient come together, put inside the water and let it boiled.

Then put inside all the vegetable and coconut milk. Let is simmer in medium heat.

After the broth simmering put inside sea salt, sugar and pepper. Then give it a taste, corrected accordingly.

Lastly put inside the coriander stalk for adding extra fragrance.

Ready to serve with warm rice and sprinkle of coriander leaves. I add some fried shallot to mine.

VEGAN CHICKEN FAJITA

This recipe are work nice when you don't have time, when you feel lazy, when you hungry and wanting something quick and not really bad meal.

I don't know if I should consider this meal as instant meal, because I used seasoning mix from package he-he. So the key here is you need to find good quality and delicious fajita mix spice. I Love the fajita mix because of this distinctive Smokey exotic flavor, and I enjoy it with warm steam rice also slice avocado. Fulfilling for hungry stomach, not too bad meal and easy lazy effort.

I used the "Fake Chicken" because that is what I have in fridge, but you could used any other option according to you preference, say button mushroom, any kind of mushroom, tofu, tempeh, or maybe even garbanzo or other tough veggies.

But here we are the dumb easy recipe.

VEGAN CHICKEN FAJITA

INGREDIENTs

1/2 onion or 1 shallot (I choose shallot though), slice it 1/2 paprika, slice it

1 scallion, slice it

250 gram fake chicken, or used the substitute 1 tbsp. ready to used fajita mix spice

Sea Salt and pepper 1 tbsp. vegetable oil

HOW TO

In medium heat and medium size pan, put inside the vegetable oil, shallot, slice paprika and the white part of the scallion, sautéed until soft and fragrance.

After the basic seasonings are fragrance, put inside the fake chicken or the substitute, continue sautéed until the fake chickens slightly change in color.

Then put in fajita spice mix, sea salt and pepper. Continue to stir, thoroughly. Don't forget to give it a taste and corrected it accordingly. Lastly put inside the green part of the scallion, stir one more time and take out from the heat.

Ready the be enjoy. See how fast this lazy meal and I enjoy it with steam rice and sprinkle of fried shallot, what a joke. Sorry Mexican.

Snow white soup

This is comfort food for us in any season, cold or hot season, in cold season it offered warm blanket of comfort, while in hot season it offered freshness and simplicity of deliciousness.

This seriously humble soup are my favorite, cheap, nutritious, easy to make and delicious.

Maybe because it brought a lot of my childhood memories, there are sentiments in this dish.

I named this "snow white soup" , I named food in weird way to attract excitement and interest of my kids even though I am being blessed that they loves veggies.

Sometime it is just silly thing to do, to laugh together with them. We are quite weird anyway, there are no boundaries for us, like placing certain food into categories, "only food to eat" on breakfast, lunch or dinner. We eat what we want, whenever we want, but only when we are hungry.

Here are the full of sentiment recipe.

Snow white soup

Ingredients

2 garlic, crush and chop roughly

1 big shallot (I choose French shallot, that what available here), slice it

1 red chili, seed out and slice (really optional, I put this chili for cold season to infused warmness)

1 small daikon radish, slice it

8 to 10 pcs of Napa cabbage, slice it roughly 2 scallions, slice it rough

500 ml water

500 ml thin coconut milk Sea salt and pepper

Sugar (adjust according your preference) 1 tbsp. vegetables oil

How to

In medium heat and medium size pot, put inside vegetable oil, chili, garlic and shallot, sautéed until soft.

After it soft, put inside water and coconut milk, let it simmer.

After the water and coconut milk are simmering put the seasoning, sea salt, pepper and sugar (I usually put sea salt and sugar with 2:1 ratio, but everything would be differ by your preference) at this point don't forget to give the stock a taste and corrected it accordingly.

Then put the cabbage and radish in, cooked until it soft but not overcooked for textured (I cooked 3-5 minute, Napa cabbage is sweet and delicious enough even when it raw).

Lastly put in the scallion and cooked for another 2 minute.

We enjoy it with warm steam rice, or just eat it as it is with sprinkle of fried onion.

Yummy

Note: you can add tofu or mushroom or carrot

Basic Indonesian sambal

There is nothing more Indonesian than this, we called it "Terong-tempe sambal penyet" or Eggplant and tempe squeezed in sambal. Yummy.. Spicy sunday morning.

Indonesian have many version of sambal, but this are the most simple, easy and versatile one. For any leftover, keep it in a fridge and it would be suitable for Indonesian nasi goreng, Indonesian mie goreng, sambal goreng with tempe, tofu or potatoes as a main ingredient. Most of the time, I made in big batch and store most of them in a fridge.

Sambal always able to awaken my appetite, not saying that I don't like eating, sometime when I really get bored and don't want to eat anything complicated, or don't have any energy to cooked one (the complicated one), sambal will always there and work for me.

Only sambal and warm rice, with rice cracker too, I feel so rich ha-ha, it is so easy and cheap to please me.

Here is the recipe

Basic Indonesian sambal

INGREDIENTs

3 medium shallot, roughly slice it 2 garlic, roughly slice it

1 small ripe tomatoes roma (any tomatoes with thin flesh), quartered.

1-2 red chili (or any amount depend on your spicy palette, deseed or keep the seed, do what you prefer), slice

2-3 hot bird eyes chili (or omit this), slice 2 tbsp. of vegetable oil

I tsp. sugar 1/2 tsp. salt

How to

In medium pan and medium heat put inside 1 tbsp. oil and put the chili, garlic, shallot in, fried them until soft and slightly brown.

Take them out and put it in pestle and mortar.

Put inside remaining oil and tomatoes into the pan on medium heat, fried until the edge of the tomatoes are golden and I dare you to pushed it into slightly burn.

While waiting the tomatoes golden, grind the garlic, shallot and chili roughly, season with salt and sugar.

Lastly, after the tomatoes are golden put it inside of pestle and mortar, grind roughly and thoroughly together with the other ingredient.

And it is done.

Note: For fried tempe, I dried rub the tempe with dried garlic, dried parsley and salt, left it for 10-15 minute then fried it in hot oil until golden.

For the eggplants, 1 medium eggplant, slice it then just fried it 1-2 tbs of oil until it burn and Smokey.

Just squeeze them in the sambal, and enjoy it with lettuce or cucumber and most importantly warm steam rice. I serve them with my favourite salad leafy green rocket (arugula) which I grow in my tiny window sill.

Traditionally Indonesian also eats them with things call "Lalap", which is basically bunch of raw vegetable. Traditional Indonesian are healthy, some said we would survive living on jungle because we eat a lot of leafy green ha-ha. It is only a joke though.

SIMPLE BUTTERNUT SQUASH SOUP

As autumn is my favorite season, this season I am going bubbling non-stop about autumn, and I am sorry. It is really autumn when you able to sight pumpkin anywhere you go, and you cannot help to not pick one of them and serve it in your table, or maybe this is only in my case.

I cannot control fresh vegetable and myself to not buy one of these seasonal, cheap when they are in season. Even though eventually I am going to delay myself to cooked it *sigh, until the time of "You have to cook it now, or you going to waste it" come in to my eyes. So super hyperbolic he-he. But it is true, this butternut squash are sitting for ages in my kitchen, I want to have some soup but just keep delay it.

And finally, the time is come. This recipe are dead easy and only required few ingredient, simple for me also have a meaning if I don't need to supervise the cooking process all the time, only don't fall a sleep he-he.

I used cream made from coconut, I usually used cream from soy or oat based, and the coconut gave a slightly tropical flavor. I cannot find proper smoke paprika in Jakarta, in Madrid luckily I able to find good, artisan one. I already compare the taste between industrial and artisan smoke paprika and the flavor different are huge, so If you have an access into artisan smoke

paprika used one, I used spicy one instead of sweet one, to kick my lazy morning ass he-he.

In this recipe to add some freshness, I also used fresh cilantro paste, the blend of spicy warm soup and tangy fresh cilantro are something. I still tried to learn and explored, contradicted flavor and textured, so far no disaster in my kitchen, yet he-he.

Chapter Nine

LIGHT COCONUT MILK CURRY

So shall we?

x

SERVE 3-4 small portions INGREDIENTs

500-gram butternut squash, without skin. Cube it quite small to fasten cooking process.

1/2 medium size sweet onion

2 big garlic cloves

1 red chili, seed in. Slice it rough

2 spring onion, only take the white part of it. Keep the green for the cilantro paste

500 ml vegetable stock

100 ml tick coconut cream

Sea salt and pepper to season, with generous amount of pepper

1 tbsp. olive oil

•

Cilantro paste (blend below ingredient together, if you have extra keep it in refrigerator, in bottle with tight lid)

Bunch hand-full of cilantro, stalk and leaves in 1 big garlic clove

1 green chili, seed in

The leftover of green part spring onion 1 tbsp. fresh lemon juice

1/2 cup extra virgin olive oil

Chapter Ten

MUSHROOM IN BARBECUE SAUCE

HOW TO

In medium size pot and medium high heat, put inside the onion, garlic, chili, and white part of spring onion. Sautéed until fragrance and the garlic slightly golden.

Put inside the butternut squash, sautéed for a while then put inside the vegetable stock. Continue cooking until the squash are soft.

Season with sea salt and pepper, and then continue to put in the coconut cream. Give a taste and corrected accordingly, continue to cook just until boiled. Take out from the heat, and blend with blender until smooth silky.

Ready to serve, I drizzle mine with the cilantro paste.

(Smoke grilled tofu)

My complete plate of happiness, this are my really bad joke "who need a therapist if you can have this full meal of happiness".

To cook this maybe you need sometime, this might be suitable for your weekend meal, because I put quite a lot of side dishes, the recipe is the next chapter and also I bake some sweet potatoes. The good news are, now I kind a found how to replace my sweet soy sauce.

I am not going to talk much about this recipe, but my trick are find good quality firm tofu, smoke one if possible since it really rich in flavor. I am lucky I got some organic smoke firm tofu to devour.

MY DIGESTION AID (Smoke grilled tofu)

Serve 2 portions INGREDIENTs

150 gram smoke firm tofu, slice it 1 cm thick (Marinate in below sauce for at least 1 hour)

For the marinated (this below can used as replacement of sweet soy sauce):

1 tsp. garlic powder 1/4 cup light soy sauce

1 tbsp. organic stevia syrup 1 tsp. smoke liquid

HOW TO

After the tofu's are well-marinated, grilled in very high heat pan, until it browning in both side.

Serve it with bake potatoes and spinach-mushroom stir-fried.

I serve this recipe with some mashed avocado with capers, super easy to make it, half avocado, 1/2 tsp. capers and 2-3 dried chili (the spicy one). Mashed avocado with capers put 1/2 tsp. of capers juice then sprinkle with dried chili

SPINACH AND MUSHROOM IN SESAME OIL AND GARLIC – AUTUMNAL EASY BREAKFAST

Here I am, enjoying breakfast, big ass garlicky breakfast, my suggestion is you need to brush your teeth afterward ;), but I tell you this breakfast are totally worth the pain.

Warming up here, I enjoy the plate with sprinkle of spicy hot chili powder, a gift from a friend which just came back from India, so thoughtful of she was gave me a pocket full of this hotness *stay focus.

This recipe is so easy, if you are grumpy and wanted to have something that quick to light up your morning then that is it. I was just drop my kids and wanting something fresh and easy, chop some garlic, heat the pan, under 15 minute and I am ready to dive, as long as you already prepare some slice mushroom and pack of fresh spinach (I choose big leaves spinach for texture since baby spinach are so mushy) then everything will be easy. I think, I can have this big plate for anytime, over breakfast, lunch, dinner, I don't mind ;).

Shall we?

SPINACH AND MUSHROOM IN SESAME OIL AND GARLIC – AUTUMNAL EASY BREAKFAST

Serve 1 Big plate INGREDIENTs

3 big cloves of garlic, chop it rough

250gram big leaves spinach (I know, that is a lot) 6 champignon mushroom, slice

1 tbsp. vegan butter 1 tbsp. sesame oil

For optional fragrance, chop some of celery leaves Sea salt and white pepper to taste

HOW TO:

Heat medium size pan under medium heat, put the butter and garlic, fried until the garlic turn golden (golden, not burn he-he).

Put inside the mushroom, sautéed until a bit soft then put inside the spinach, season quickly with sesame oil, salt and pepper.

Stir quickly to prevent the spinach turn mushy and take off from the heat.

Ready to serve, I serve mine with avocado and sprinkle of chili powder.

PENICILIN SPICE SOUP

My husband just got back from working trip, got home with really severe cold. Usually he always be the last standing when we had flu-war, he have really good immune system, so going home being knock down it is time to go get some good bowl of warm medicine soup. Similar as me, chemical medicine always our last option, not that we are anti-modern medicine but we prefer our body fight out while we devour something nutritious, good idea isn't it?

• This soup is full of spice, maybe would be remind you of warm winter December, I have ginger, nutmeg, clove and sweet cinnamon. While for the main ingredient I keep everything basic and hearty, your daily standard staple I believe. But sure you can put vegetable you'd love,

the star of this recipe are the broth.

I am not going to talk and talk, so let's go.

PENICILIN SPICE SOUP

Serve 3-4 portions INGREDIENTs

3 Carrot, slice it in chunk

3 medium potatoes, slice it in chunk 2 celery stalk, slice in in chunk

3 fat clove of garlic, crush it 5 cloves

1 cinnamon stick

1/2 small nutmeg, just put it inside whole 1 thumb size ginger, slice it

2-3 stalk parsley, slice it

Handful of green bean, slice it as you prefer 3-4 shiitake mushroom, slice it

Sea salt and pepper (a lot of it)

1 tsp. sugar (brown sugar if you like it) 1500ml water

HOW TO

In big pot and medium heat, put inside the entire ingredient together, except (slice parsley, green bean and shiitake, put them lastly before taking off from the heat).

Let the vegetable cooked slowly and soft, give proper taste (because potatoes are prone to absorb salt so maybe you need to keep check on how the broth are taste).

When everything please you put inside the last ingredients, and cooked for couple of minutes, 5-8 minute,

Take off from heat and ready to serve.

I serve mine with fried shallot, this was splendidly satisfying.

FOOD FOR MIND

This are food for my mind, as I told you before, I used food as my conveyance of live so this recipe are literally for my mind. I have quite bad anxiety, which I notice when I was un-nurtured, my body, I got anxious pretty easily and it will continue getting bad. I tried this kind of easy food for quite sometime, it help me through difficult time, or I think so or maybe I could deceive my mind by think it so. This natural remedy are worked quite well for me, for temporary at least he- he but it much better than taking any chemical medicine, don't you think so?

• This are simple recipe, I only used ginger, garlic, black pepper and Himalayan salt to seasoned, the amount of ginger I used is only 2 slice as I don't want it to over power the flavor, I just want an infuse of warmness, for the rest I let the ingredient do the talking. I always have shiitake in my fridge when it in season, as I love it for my emergency ingredient, it is versatile in

everything and it taste super delicious.

The warm hint of ginger, the sweetness of petit pois (just green peas, as we called it in Spanish Guisantes), the chewy savory of shiitake and salty spinach, do I need to describe it even more? I enjoy this meal with my fried rice, if you don't get bored with my fried rice I will attach the recipe here, it is caramelize onion, lime leaves and lemon grass fried rice, quite odd combo but I love it, it is fragrance.

So shall we?

FOOD FOR MIND VEGETABLE STIR FRIED SERVE 1 PORTION

INGREDIENTs

100 gram frozen spinach (this become my standard kitchen staple) 1/2-cup petit pois or baby green peas.

3 shiitake mushroom, slice it 1 tbsp. sesame oil

2 thin slice of ginger

2 fat garlic, crush and chop Himalayan salt and black pepper

HOW TO

In medium pan and high heat, put inside the sesame oil, garlic and ginger, sautéed for a while and keep an eye, don't burn them, continue to bring in shiitake, sautéed until fragrance.

Then put in the spinach and petit pois, season with Himalayan salt and black pepper. Give a taste, corrected according your preference.

When everything is perfectly please you, take out from the heat.

CARAMELIZED ONION FRIED RICE

SERVE 2 small portions INGREDIENTs

2 cup or small bowl of cold cooked rice

1 sweet onion, slice (I prefer sweet onion, since I can not take yellow or other onion, but you can do as your preferred)

4 kefir lime leaf

lemon grass, crush the white part 2 fat garlic

tbsp. sweet soy sauce

1 tsp. vegetable stock powder 1 tbsp. sesame oil

Himalayan salt and black pepper HOW TO

In medium pan and high heat, put inside the sesame oil, garlic and slice sweet onion, sautéed until the onion, are soft sweating and fragrance, then put inside the lime leaf and lemon grass, continue to stirred until you can smell the fragrance of lime and lemon grass.

Put inside the rice and stirred it well, continue to put in the rest of seasoning (salt, pepper, sweet soy sauce and vegetable stock powder), be careful on how much you put your salt, better to put it little by little as there are a lot of saltines factor here.

Continue to stir in high heat, until you can smell smoky flavor. Then take out from the heat.

You can serve it right away, or you can serve like mine with vegetable stir fried above, slice of avocado and sprinkle of chili flake.

TOFU SEAWEED SOUP THAI STYLE

This quite unusual combo, but the heat will be warmed your cold stomach and maybe your cold heart too *sigh.

Initially I have difficulty to choose, do I want to make red Thai curry or Tom yam soup, which is quite interesting to do both, Ohm I feel being torn *fainting dramatically, seem like my tantrum doesn't heal yet he-he.

Finally I choose to have Red Thai curry which I enjoy with my daughter, She got cold for almost a week, the heat are warming his stomach and I tried to make her comfortable by food, she also big fan of sea weed. We enjoy it as out second breakfast *he-he.

I want to make it another bowl for my lunch tomorrow, yup you hear me tomorrow, it is quick to make as long as you have Red Thai curry paste, I always have good quick paste in my fridge just in case. Also did quite fridge foraging actually, I know that I want to have tofu and seaweed but my fat Shiitake also caught my eyes so I put them too, it is like ocean of warm umami.

Chapter Eleven

MY DIGESTION AID

So shall we have a dinner?

x

Serve 2 small bowls INGREDIENTs

1 Tbsp. good red Thai curry paste 2 shiitake mushroom, slice it

1 tbsp. dried wakame seaweed (this will be become good enough amount for this recipe, this dried wakame usually already in small shape in one bite size)

2-3 cherry tomatoes, slice in a half

70 gram firm dice tofu (you absolutely can add some more)

tsp. vegetable bouillon or replace the water in this recipe with vegetable stock. 2 cup water or vegetable stock

1/2 cup thick coconut milk 3-4 stalk cilantro

spring onion, slice it rough Sea salt and pepper to taste

1 tbsp. vegetable oil HOW TO

In small medium saucepan and medium heat, put inside the vegetable and red Thai curry paste, stir awhile until fragrance, but becareful not to burn them (mine was almost burn).

Put inside the vegetable stock or the water continue with tofu, let them boiled.

After it boiling put inside the coconut milk and the rest of the ingredient, let them boiled once again then take them out from the heat. Don't forget to give them a taste and corrected accordingly.

Ready to serve, I serve mine with slice avocado and cilantro stalk (I put avocado on everything just for you to know he-he).

OYSTER MUSHROOM WITH SPICY SMOKY

PAPRIKA

Is not usually very cold in here, winter come early this year. Even quite lucky though, I still found a lot of mushroom and cheap *jejeje (laughing in Spanish), I love cheap delicious food. So bear with me, I am going to post a lot of mushroom recipe.

I start noticing my habitual eating are changing, I eat even more often than usual *jejeje, in small portion though, in my defend, even though there are nothing wrong about love to eat, I eat consciously *my another defend he-he.

This recipe are easy, light enough for snacking. I consider this as my solitary indulgence, I have it for my pre-lunch snacking, yes, there is such thing as pre-lunch *je-je, when I am alone at home. On my solitary time, I love to try something random to eat, this are one of the result of my solitary time.

For seasoning, I put things as minimal and basic as possible, and let my smoky paprika to stand out. I bought this smoky paprika quite sometime ago, this were artisan where it hand made, the flavor are quite different, strong and mellow in the same time. So if you have one in hand

please used it, if not just used smoke paprika you have in hand (mild or spicy one, according of your preference)

So, shall we have some solitary indulgence?

OYSTER MUSHROOM WITH SPICY SMOKY PAPRIKA

Serve 1 portion INGREDIENT

100-150 gram fresh oyster mushroom (choose the firm one, and shredded)

11/2 tsp. smoke paprika (I choose the spicy one)

1/2 tsp. garlic powder

1/2 tsp. dried parsley

1/2 ground white pepper

Sea salt to taste (I just used 1/2 tsp. approximately)

1 tbsp. regular olive oil

Few spring of parsley to serve (I don't bother to chop it, I just user scissor je-je) Note: if you love, you can have some toast to serve it. As pre-lunch or breakfast

HOW TO

In one big plate, mixed all the ingredients together, mixed well until the mushroom are covered with seasoning.

In one medium pan and medium high heat (ensure the pan are very hot, it is important to have hot pan here, we want to emerge and enhance smokiness of the paprika). Put inside the mushroom in batch (I have mine in two batches), don't over crowd the mushroom).

After you done with the entire batch, it is ready to serve. Sprinkle with chop parsley.

If you would like, you can have some toast to serve. I just ate as it is.

Chapter Twelve

VEGAN ZUCCHINI NOODLE TOM YAM

At first I thought quite complicated to create one, but after experience it myself, it was quite easy, all you need is fresh ingredient, when you got one, you will get perfect meal. Enjoy this dishes while it hot, it was quite experience, I was once taste a good tom yam in Thailand, when you got everything almost perfect even in the street and this recipe is worthy for every mess.

I am not going too long and too much talk here; let's have a life

SERVE 2 generous portions

MUSHROOM IN BARBECUE SAUCE

Serve 2 for filling with hotdog bun / 1 portion INGREDIENTs

NOTE: The basic seasoning and ingredient are as I write in previous chapter, here

1 tbsp. regular olive oil

1 shallot or 1/2 onion, slice

1 tbsp. whole grain mustard

2 tbsp. tomatoes sauce

3 tbsp. barbecue sauce

Note: you also can serve it with your favorite bun. HOW TO

After you prepare mushroom as previous chapter, set aside the mushroom.

In the same pan and medium high heat, put inside the olive oil and shallot,

sautéed until shallots are caramelize.

Put inside the rest of the ingredient and stir it well.

Give a taste and corrected according your preference. Then put inside the mushroom, stir sometime until the sauce are coating the mushroom well.

Take it out from the heat.

I serve mine with sweet bun and another extra mustard, but I also ate some of them as it is. You also can serve them with gherkin, jalapeño or some lettuce.

herb and vegetable, that is how I express life, interesting and intriguing in many way *sigh ha- ha.INGREDIENTs

100 gram zucchini noodle

5-6 slice fried tofu

2 Portobello mushrooms, slice it

1 medium tomatoes, slice it chunk

1 tbsp. Thai chili paste (put 2 tbsp. if you love spicy and thick broth)

1 small size of onion, slice it

2 garlic clove, slice it

3 lemon grass, take the white part and slice it

5 kaffir lime leaves, shredded to emerge the fragrance

2 chunk slice of galangal

6 bird eye chili (add more if you love spicy)

Juice from 2 lime (add more if you like more sour)

750ml vegetable stock

1 tsp. sea salt

1 tsp. brown sugar

Handful of coriander leaves HOW TO

In medium size pot and medium high heat, put inside the vegetable stock and Thai chili paste, boiled them.

When the stock are boiling, put inside the herb (lemon grass, onion, garlic, galangal, lime leaves, and chili), put the stock boiling again, then season with salt and sugar, give a taste and adjust it according your preference.

When the stocks are perfect, put inside the zucchini noodle, slice tomatoes, mushroom and tofu, then cooked them for 2-3 minute.

Lastly before off from the heat put inside half coriander (just tear it roughly) and lime juices, give a taste again to adjust the sourness.

Serve it while hot and sprinkle with the extra coriander.

CPSIA information can be obtained
at www.ICGtesting.com
Printed in the USA
LVHW060108020522
717671LV00035B/825